Women, Do You Know What You Really Want?

Andrea DiMattia; Loretta Becker

authorHOUSE®

AuthorHouse™
1663 Liberty Drive
Bloomington, IN 47403
www.authorhouse.com
Phone: 1 (800) 839-8640

Published by AuthorHouse 07/20/2016

ISBN: 978-1-5246-1456-0 (sc)
ISBN: 978-1-5246-1455-3 (e)

Library of Congress Control Number: 2016909811

Print information available on the last page.

Acknowledgments

To all the women in our lives—past, present, and future—thank you for being friends, lovers, and life teachers. The laughter and joy will remain stamped in our hearts forever. Namaste.

Nothing is perfect. Life is messy. Relationships are complex. Outcomes are uncertain. People are irrational.

—Hugh Mackay

What Do You Want In a Partner?

I don't need a perfect woman; I just need a perfect woman for me.

Ask yourself what you are looking for in a relationship.

Are you looking for a life partner, casual dating, or a just a good time?

How do we view the people that we date?

Are we feeling desire, need, or want?

Desire is defined as "a strong feeling of wanting to have something or wishing something to happen." We all have desires. What is it that you desire? Examples would be: I desire a girlfriend, someone I can call my own; she is beautiful, smart, funny, has an hourglass body. I am the only one she sees; she is faithful. I am her one and only. I will be with her for the rest of my life.

Are these realistic and healthy desires?

Need is defined as a "circumstance in which something is necessary or that requires some course of action." I need to be in a relationship. I cannot be alone. How will I spend my time, and what will I do? What will others think of me if I am alone? What do I think of myself? Am I not worthy? Is something wrong with me? Am I not likeable and lovable? Is all this worrying about my ego healthy thinking?

Lastly, there is what we would consider the healthy option, *want*. Want is defined as the desire to possess or do (something). This is possible if you are confident, have a strong sense of self and are secure. Do you want a long term relationship with depth? If you want a relationship with depth, then you must

1

be intentional about how you are choosing the women that you date.

Inner reflection and your own personal experiences will assist you in deciding what attributes are valuable to you in a significant other. Intelligence, wisdom, and a sense of fun are all long-lasting character traits. What might you be looking for in a woman? Is she a scholar or master of life lessons? Looks fade but inner beauty remains for a lifetime. Is she a genuine person? A person who is authentic, sincere, and honest? Is she ready to build a foundation in a relationship that includes friendship, partnership, and relating as a lover?

If your desires, needs, and wants are not balanced, you must figure out what it is that you are searching for. Is there something missing from you emotionally? Accepting yourself for who you are and being comfortable in your own skin are both prerequisites for healthy and successful dating. Think about what you need to do to be successful in building a healthy relationship.

Where do you find the girl next door? Is she a click away?

The profile-building begins as you go online and visit various dating websites.

Do dating sites really identify what you are looking for when you answer the profile questions and read someone's profile? How many questions and profiles does it take to get to the center of her Tootsie Pop?

Online dating uses a web-based forum that provides a safe place for individuals to make contact and communicate with each other for a personal pleasure or a romantic, and/or sexual relationship (Finkel, Eastwick, Karney, Reis, and Sprecher, 2012; Houran, 2006). The prospective member provides personal information and searches the online service's database for individuals using criteria such as age, gender, and location.

Examples of online dating services include Match.com and Eharmony.

As a prospective member responds to questions in the profile survey, the program searches for compatible links in its database. Imagine yourself filling out one of these surveys; it's important as you answer the questions to be truly honest—rather than answering the way you think that others may find appealing. Why not tell the truth? Imagine! You might meet the woman who is perfect for you! If you stretch the truth and create a persona that is false, you must be cautious. When you meet, the bubble will burst, and your date will think, *Who is this person?* That can generate major trust issues, and no healthy relationship can be built on a foundation of untruth.

When putting yourself out there, it is only fair to be certain that your last relationship is truly in the past and that you are emotionally ready to date someone new. Give yourself time after a breakup, and know where you are emotionally; be sure that you are able to leave her in the past. If you honestly feel that you are emotionally ready, then go ahead and move forward with dating. If not, state in your profile that you are seeking friends only.

Why? Think how you would feel. How often have you met someone who talks constantly about her ex? Or she is still referring to her ex as a *"friend"* in a way that doesn't appear to allow her to enter into a new relationship.

Once, while I was online looking to date, I chatted and e-mailed with a woman who had only been broken up for four weeks from her girlfriend of a couple of years. She revealed that she and the ex-girlfriend wanted to get back together. I wished her well and told her that if she could fix her relationship that would be great; the grass isn't always greener. Four days later, she called me to say it didn't work out—and asked whether I would still like to go out with her. I did not go. I didn't enjoy feeling like I was her second choice. Most importantly for me, I didn't know where she was emotionally regarding dating.

And another thing about an ex—she is your ex for a reason; that relationship did *not* work! So be in the present. Learn from your past relationships (send them light and love)—and move forward.

Online dating is not the way to fill a void of loneliness, hardship, or sex. You must finish one chapter before you move forward to the next. All the way, you will be growing, processing, and feeling your emotions before moving on to the next relationship.

She's got Personality! **What kind of personality are you searching for?**

Do you like to laugh? Is your cup half full or half empty? Do you wake up with a smile on your face? Are you a coffee and conversation kind of woman, or do you like the atmosphere quiet, with minimal conversation? Are you artistic; do you enjoy music, culture, and the arts? Do you prefer a woman who has similar cultural interests? Are you athletic? Do you like to go sky diving, deep water fishing, white water rafting? Again, what do you like and want? Do you want a compatible partnership that splits things 50-50, creating a balance that is Ying and Ying? Do you get attracted to someone who is your opposite and balances your traits? There is no reason for you to settle. For every Jill there is another Jill. If you do not find her right away keep going online. If at first you don't succeed look, click and search again.

What is your preference regarding appearance?

Do you like butch, fem, androgynous, transsexual—or everything in between? Only you can answer that one. Remember to be honest with yourself, and start your journey off right!

Always look below the surface—beyond her looks. What else is appealing in a relationship?

Looks don't define a person. Beauty is skin deep, as they say, and always in the eyes of the beholder.

I met a beautiful woman once that I thought was the woman of my dreams. She had the body of a model and a beautiful face. Quickly, though, through conversation, I learned that she wasn't so nice, and she couldn't hold a conversation that was of interest or intellect. Later, I met a woman who is full-figured, funny, nice, and intelligent. My interest was piqued, and now she is my image of a true beauty!

Keep in mind that your first impression may not be a lasting one; you may want to keep an open mind regarding appearances.

In online dating, for some, not being able to view someone's photo is a deal-breaker, and for others, the picture is irrelevant. Keep in mind that looks can sometimes be deceiving.

Self-Reflections

What Do You Want In a Partner?

- List your desires, needs, and wants.

  _____

  _____

  _____

- What attributes are you looking for?

  _____

  _____

  _____

  _____

- In building your profile, want do you want her to know about you?

  _____

  _____

  _____

  _____

- What are your preferences regarding appearance?

  _____

  _____

  _____

  _____

Distance

How far is too far?

For some people distance is very important. Are you willing to drive an hour to see each other? If not, how far are you willing to go? Are you willing to do half the driving? What happens if things get serious and you want to spend more and more time together?

Depending on your tolerance for travel, time, and distance, this element may have no effect on your dating experience, but it is definitely something to consider.

After a few dates, you'll probably have a couple of questions: where are you in the relationship, and how often do you want to see each other?

Keeping in mind your careers, lifestyles, children, and family responsibilities, you'll both need to decide what is an acceptable amount of time spend together. Life gets in the way. At the beginning of a relationship, an adequate amount of time is needed. Is it once a week? Weekends-only or several times a week? Do you establish set days that you see each other? Or do you keep it casual?

Moving forward with an open mind will allow the relationship to develop while still maintaining individual friendships and personal space. Know yourself; how much of that "me" time do you need to prevent suffocation?

Self-Reflections

Distance

- How far are you willing to drive?

  _____

  _____

  _____

- How much time do you want to spend together?

  _____

  _____

  _____

Age Differences

What age range are you seeking?

Does age matter in a relationship? Do you date a woman your age, older, or younger? What is your preference regarding the age difference with a partner?

Your own age may play a role when choosing women to date. Are you active, and do you want a woman with the same stamina? If so, you may want a woman a few years younger. Will you be able to relate to each other so there isn't an obvious generation gap or lack of physical attraction?

If you date an older woman, this may work for you in the beginning, but will her appearance, interests, and emotional and physical attraction decline as the years pass and she ages?

These may be some questions to ask yourself. How do you think about the person you are dating—now and in the long term? For example, if you are thirty-two and date a fifty-two-year-old, the relationship might be okay now. But what about when you are a healthy, active fifty-two-year-old and your girlfriend is seventy-two and asking for her senior citizen discount when you go out? Do you see an aged woman?

When I was twenty-three, I dated a woman thirteen years older. She is still a very dear friend of mine. Six years into the relationship, age became an issue. At this point, I was twenty-nine and she was forty-two. Examples of the things that could be classified as generational differences were our taste in music, our varied sexual experiences, and being in the closet versus being a very "out" lesbian. I was feeling the age difference in our views regarding life as well, and I wanted a partner closer to my age.

For example, I once was in the process of talking and connecting online with a woman who was twelve years my senior. I was very interested in meeting her despite the age gap. We communicated well. I had given myself a twelve-year age range on my dating profile and felt it was acceptable for me. We decided to meet at a halfway point. As I got out of the car, she stated, "You look like you could be a lot of fun." Over dinner, we had great intellectual conversation and decided we would meet again. I left feeling unsure about how I truly felt about the age difference. I felt like we connected intellectually, but her physical appearance was older, as were her mannerisms. After the date, I changed my profile age range to an eight-year gap. We spoke again and realized we would be better off as friends, and we still speak on occasion.

Looks fade, and you are left with her being. Can you live with that? Is she still the woman of your dreams? If you anticipate that any of these things would be a problem for you, then age should be a serious consideration in choosing whom to date.

Self-Reflections

Age

- Does age play a factor?

  _____
  _____

- What age range do you want?

  _____
  _____
  _____

Size

Does size matter?

What is your weight preference in a woman—thin or more voluptuous? Do you want a woman with all the right curves? Whatever your preferences, please do not say, "Why don't you lose fifty pounds? Then I will sleep with you." This has happened to me. I admit I am not a small person, but if this is not your preference, don't ask me out on four dates and then inquire if I am thinking about working out and losing some weight. Who says that? Weight is a personal preference, but it is not all there is to a person.

As a woman who struggles with her weight, I prefer a woman who is thinner than I am. My curves are usually more than ample, and my partners have preferred larger woman, so it works.

Self-Reflections

Size

- What is your personal preference?

_____

_____

_____

Chatting and E-Mailing

When meeting someone new, how do you capture her interest? What goes into the first hello, the art of selling yourself?

Knowing what you are looking for while reviewing profiles is an important first step in online dating. It is all about enticing someone with similar interests or it's an effort to attract someone with a specific personality, a compatible lifestyle, and interest in the same types of activities.

Initial chats or e-mails can include requests and questions alike. "Tell me about yourself. What do you like to do? Is your idea of fun being outdoors and camping by a fire, or do you prefer getting a room and staying at a high end hotel? How do you want to attract the bee to your honey?"

Once her profile has piqued your interest, the next step is letting her know. Do you wink, chat, send an e-mail? What is your style, comfort level, and amount of confidence? These are individual preferences and depend on how you feel about dating and your perception of her profile. Some people find the process of dating to be intimidating and nerve-racking, while others thoroughly enjoy the process of getting to know new people through dating. Your point-of-view will influence how you choose to move forward. If you are timid or shy, you may want to start off slowly.

When do you ask for her phone number? Who makes the first call? Are you worried about sharing your number with a stranger? If you have concerns with her and it does not feel right then stop. That is a red flag. You have to be intuitive; trust your "sixth sense"—and truly listen to what she is saying. Be present and capture nuances of her personality. If you are comfortable, then continue and give your phone number or ask for hers. Remember, someone has to take the first step. Be brave!

With the first phone call, the dating dance and "courtship" continues. I would hope that, by now, you feel like you have danced with two steps forward because the conversation has flowed and you have established a good comfort level on the phone. Some conversation starters you could try follow here:

- **How would you like to start our conversation?**
- **Would you like me to start or you?**
- **Tell me about yourself**?
    - What interests do you have?
    - Do you like to travel?
    - What do you do for fun/leisure time?
- **Tell me about your family?**
    - Do you have children?
- **What do you do for work?**

When you hang up, insecurities and worry may set in, and you may wonder whether she liked you. It might feel like the dance went one step backward. Stay confident, and remember that this is part of the dating process. If this woman does not call you, don't give up on yourself and try not to take it personally. It is sometimes impossible to know where the other person is in her own dating process. Take each interaction as a learning experience. You know what you have to bring to a relationship, and when the right woman comes along, she will know it too.

Self-Reflections

Chatting and E-Mailing

- How will you pique her interest?

  _____

  _____

  _____

  _____

- What will pique your interest?

  _____

  _____

  _____

  _____

- E-mailing, reaching out by winking or chatting—what are you comfortable with?

  _____

  _____

  _____

  _____

- When should you ask for her phone number?

  _____

  _____

  _____

  _____

Meet and Greet

Where do you want to meet, and under what circumstances? Dating websites suggest safety guidelines, such as letting someone know where you are meeting and at what time. Keep a cell phone with you, and meet in a public place.

Do you meet for a drink, coffee, or a light meal? On a first meeting, we suggest that you meet at a halfway point, if there is a distance.

So you've met, and the first date went well. The awkward moment occurs and one of you asks, "Would you like to spend more time together?"

If you are not into each other, be honest and say. "I enjoyed meeting with you, but I am not interested in seeing you again."

Keep in mind that her feelings could get hurt. Be kind and polite, and remember that dating can be difficult for one's self esteem. Thus being honest is important!

Self-Reflections

Meet and Greet

- Where will you meet?

  _____

  _____

  _____

- Will there be a second date?

  _____

  _____

  _____

  _____

The Dating Journey Begins

How much do you share during the first few conversations? Are you interviewing her as you are getting to know her? Are you keeping a mental log of how she responds to your questions? We all tend to do this.

In one of our first conversations, a girlfriend told me she had come out of a twelve-year relationship and she had only been single for four months. My first thought was, *Where is this girl at? Am I her rebound? Is she ready to date?*

In further discussion, she told me that she was ready to date because the relationship had already been over for a period of time. Though she was a bit apprehensive, she stated that she usually doesn't call and she prefers e-mails.

My response, point blank, was, "Why are you on a dating website?"

There was silence on the line. I thought to myself, *was I too abrupt?* I did feel very strongly about what I had said because this was a dating website—and I was not looking for a pen-pal.

In past experiences, I learned that many women enjoy the pen-pal experience, but I was done with that. She agreed with me and asked me out on a date.

When communicating with a prospective date, it is easy to fall into the trap of psychoanalyzing everything a person says.

Due to my background, I keep a running log in my head regarding things like family structure, friendships, values, and commitment. I do this with all my relationships (friends, family), including my dating encounters.

While actively dating, I kept notes on various women. I didn't want to confuse whom I was speaking with, as I was chatting online and over the phone with several women. I kept little notes on their interests, etc., since I didn't want to insult anyone. Repeating a conversation with a woman or telling the same story for a second time would make a woman believe I was insensitive or didn't remember what we had discussed. Taking notes helped me keep the stories straight.

Once, I was simultaneously chatting with four women online and set up dates to meet each of them.

- Date number one: We met at a bar and she was nothing like she had presented herself online. Online she stated she was employed; in person, she admitted that she was unemployed. Her stories didn't align with what she portrayed in our conversations or in her profile. Needless to say, we didn't have a second date.
- When I met woman number two, we got along very well. After we had several dates, though, I learned that she was living with her ex-wife, and I realized she wasn't available. I prefer a woman who is available for dating sans entanglements.
- This brings me to woman number three. We went on about four dates and then she asked to borrow some money. *Are you kidding me?* Talk about a red flag! That was the end of that.
- Woman number four lived in another state so we met at a halfway point. We had chatted at great length over the phone, but in person, she had nothing to say and was very unpleasant. Feeling very surprised and uneasy in the behavior change, I was out of there after a short period of time. There was no second date.

Without being discouraged, I said to myself, *back to the chat lines!*

My approach to interviews and dating begins with the reminder that it will unfold naturally. The key is approaching the encounter as a journey and just enjoying the experience of dating.

Find out what she likes to do for fun and decide how well that coincides with your interests and lifestyle. How well does she get along with her friends and family? What kind of work does she do? Is she financially stable?

How well does she communicate her thoughts and views? I want someone who is able to express herself without arguing her points and opinions to the point of always having to be right. What do you want?

A little psychoanalysis of yourself is okay, but try to relax and not make judgments before getting to know the person. Work on being more open to the experience and living in the moment.

Self-Reflections

The Dating Journey Begins

- How will you keep an open mind?

  _____

  _____

  _____

- Comparing her personality with yours, what is she like?

  _____

  _____

  _____

Honesty and Values

Oh what a tangled web we weave, when at first we practice to deceive.

—Sir Walter Scott

We all have a past and a history. When meeting someone, the question is how much you share in the beginning. For example, on one of my first meetings, I was frightened when the woman told me that her son had emotional problems, her brother had committed suicide, her ex-husband was gay, and she had some personal issues she wasn't ready to share that day.

At another first date, the dinner was lovely and romantic, and as the evening progressed, she shared that she had a cat whom she loved. She continued, and shared that one night she woke up to the cat sucking her breast. That was too much sharing for me! Would you choose to go on a second date after that?

Establish your boundaries and comfort levels as a way to tell whether a woman might not be the right person for you. Stand your own ground.

Is there a Spark?

Chemistry does play a significant role in dating. If you feel a spark and you think it is mutual, then you should extend the date or make plans to see each other again.

Suggestions for a next date

What are your interests? We all have an idea of the perfect date. It might be walking in the woods, visiting a quaint seaside town, or going for a drive. Depending on your interests, you may enjoy a fine arts museum then have a meal together. To show your playful side, suggest mini-golf, batting cages, or playing pool. All of these allow you both to see various sides of each other while interacting and engaging together.

One of my past dates wanted to have a very casual first meeting at an arcade, where we played air hockey and had a drink. She told me, "You play aggressive."

My response was, "I play to win." She smiled at me and asked me out again.

There is an age-old running joke: What does a lesbian bring to a second date? And the answer is a U-Haul! For some reason, most lesbians are guilty of this at some point in their life. What's up with the speed at which many lesbians date? It seems like many of us progress at the speed of lightening. As women, most of us share and communicate well, which then fosters emotional connections. We will put a bookmark on this thought, as later on we will discuss love versus infatuation (see the love chart).

Before you think of that U-Haul, get to know the other person and question why you are in this relationship. Examine your inner self to ensure that you are not entering a relationship out of "need." This is not an optimal reason to be in a relationship.

Some unhealthy examples of need include looking to share expenses (you are between jobs and or in debt) or to fill a void. If you don't like to live alone, maybe you should think about getting a roommate or a dog, not a girlfriend.

Another common situation is a relationship where the sex is great, but you argue a lot. You may be involved for the wrong reasons; sex shouldn't control the relationship. Buy a toy!

Discuss the reasons for being in the relationship and your expectations *before* you are living in the same space with this individual and getting more than you signed up for.

Is this scenario familiar: The bills are still there, the sex is getting old, and you are now arguing more than you expected.

Stop and think of your motives, and don't fall into the U-Haul trap. You may find yourself in a relationship with more debt, having no personal space, and involved with a woman you don't want! Ms. Right has now become Ms. Wrong. Take time and get to know a woman before you move in. Rome wasn't built in a day; neither are relationships.

My U-Haul nightmare involved dating a woman for only a few months. It started with her dog needing a place to stay (he bit the neighbor's dog). He lived with me for a few months before she moved in. Before I knew it, I had band equipment on my dinner table, a drum set in the dining room, black curtains in my bedroom, and a skeleton welcome mat. I thought to myself *OMG, what did I do?* The dog alone would have been enough. I politely asked her to move out after only a month. We are still friendly today.

STOP!

Not every date will be the woman of your dreams. She may not be the perfect woman for you. She may be a good friend and become part of your circle of networking. Having and making a variety of friends is an important part of building a network.

Each woman has a different reason for coming into your life—the artist, nurse, realtor, truck driver. They all can continue to be with you in a variety of capacities. She may become a best friend that leads you to Ms. Right.

People come in and out of our lives all the time for many different reasons. They make impressions and footprints on our hearts that we will carry throughout our lives. Sometimes one journey leads to the next. Enjoy the dating process, relax, and go with the flow.

Self-Reflections

Honesty and Values

- What will you share, and how do you communicate?

  _____

  _____

  _____

  _____

- Is it easy or difficult for you to stand your own ground and to be yourself? Why?

  _____

  _____

  _____

  _____

- Is there a spark or chemistry?

  _____

  _____

  _____

  _____

- Is one of you a U-Haul girl?

  _____

  _____

  _____

  _____

Defining Your Relationship

What works for the two of you?

Setting parameters for your dating experience will bring a sense of security and help you know what is expected in the relationship. Communication and a sense of security help establish a foundation for a healthy relationship.

Do you choose to date exclusively or have multiple dating partners? We each have individual expectations of how we hope the relationship will grow. These discussions should be had early on to prevent miscommunication, hurt feelings, and loss of trust. Questions to ask include the following:

- Are you dating several women presently?
- How do you feel about dating exclusively?

Self-Reflections

Defining Your Relationship

- Setting parameters: What works for you?

  _____

  _____

  _____

  _____

- Dating exclusively or multiple partners?

  _____

  _____

  _____

  _____

Substance Use

What are your personal habits around drinking and using other substances? What are you willing to live with? What if you are out on a date and you have one or two drinks, while your date is on her sixth cocktail? She is slurring her words, and her personality changes; is she Ms. Jekyll or Ms. Hyde?

What you define as a social drinker, another person may consider being a problem drinker. I once dated a woman who stated that she was a social drinker. After several months, I learned she was drinking in secret. This was not acceptable for me. What is important is to know what is comfortable for you in your own daily life.

What is your tolerance regarding recreational and prescription drug use? Consider marijuana, cocaine, ecstasy, and alcohol as well as smoking; know your own personal limits, as this has an effect on your relationship and personal life both emotionally and financially.

Self-Reflections

Substance Use

- What is your tolerance regarding alcohol and recreational drug use?

_____

_____

_____

_____

- What about smoking?

_____

_____

_____

_____

- What can you live with, and what can't you live with?

_____

_____

_____

_____

Who Pays?

"Waiter, check please!"

If you are talking about dating within a butch-fem situation, it is likely the butch would prefer to take care of the bill. A butch lesbian tends to step into a dominant role more often than not, and it is usually considered chivalrous for her to pick up the tab when escorting a date out on the town. In a fem-fem situation, we think alternating the bill works.

Practically speaking, whoever asked the other one on the date should pay the bill. If you are just friends or going out as friends, we suggest splitting the check. If you want to make a nice impression pay the tab.

Self-Reflections

Who Pays?

- How do you feel about paying the tab or taking turns?

  _____

  _____

  _____

  _____

Being Callous

Are you looking to be committed to one woman or are you casually dating. Is she just another notch in your belt; one more conquest? Presently, what are your wants, desires and needs?

Continue to rethink your responses as you view more profiles. Women are responding according to your picture and how you represent yourself.

Has cyber-dating caused you to become callous as you scan through pictures and profiles? As you scan more profiles, do you feel more detached from the individuals? Has this caused you to have a lack of sensitivity?

Try to remember that there is a real woman on the other side of that screen that has wants, desires and needs—just as you have. Remember to be mindful and respectful. The lesbian community is small, and you never know when you may meet this individual in another setting.

Self-Reflections

Being Callous

- How will you be mindful and respectful of the other person?

  _____

  _____

  _____

  _____

Dating with Children

Do you like or want children in your life? How do they fit in? There are various options. Would you want to have a child that the two of you create together? Could you love another person's child as your own?

How do you feel about dating someone who already has children? Be aware that there may be parents present on the dating websites, and the family dynamics would impact your future relationship. You would become another dynamic in this relationship, and you would need to accept the other parent the other parent of your partner's child.

I had a friend who had been in a long-term relationship. They had adopted a child together. The new partner was jealous of the parenting relationship that was already present.

Ongoing amicable and respectful communication is required to raise a well-balanced, emotionally stable child. It should not be cause for jealously. The child's best interest should always come first.

Children will have their own feelings and responses to your new relationship. Those feelings can be positive or negative and may show in their behaviors, sometimes in bad behaviors. It is always going to be the parent's job to deal with whatever issues arise. Keep in mind that this can be a sensitive topic. Kids can sometimes make or break a relationship.

Also consider the dynamics of getting to know the woman and then her child. Prior to meeting the child, it is good to establish a strong relationship with your new girlfriend. Get to know each other through dating, and build on your friendship, trust, and possibly love. You have to date and continue to get to know each other; instant families do not exist. It takes time and nurturing.

Self-Reflections

Dating with Children

- Do you want children?

_____

_____

_____

- What matters to you in getting to know each other prior to involving children?

_____

_____

_____

The Love Chart

How do I love thee? Let me count the ways …

How soon is too soon to say *I love you?*

You feel like you are on cloud nine and you are growing emotionally attached to your new girlfriend; you want to always be with her, you think about her all day long. Is this infatuation, or are you in love? How well do you know yourself?

The Love Chart

	INFATUATION	LOVE
Definition:	Infatuation is the state of being completely carried away by unreasoning desire.	A decision to commit oneself to another and to work through conflicts instead of giving up.
Associated with:	Selfish uncontrollable desire	Physical chemistry over a fairly long period of time.
Sub-Categories:	Short lived physical desire, crush, or lust, hormonal activity, addictive chemical reactions in the brain.	Intimacy, commitment, security, the desire to please and help the other person.
Symptoms:	Urgency, intensity, sexual desire, anxiety, high risk choices, reckless abandonment of what was once valued.	Faithfulness, loyalty, confidence. Willingness to make sacrifices for another. Working at settling differences.
Person to Person:	Reckless commitment to satisfy one's all consuming lust.	Commitment to another. Genuine intentions. Think about other person's feelings before acting.
Feels like:	All consuming euphoria similar to recreational drug use (addictive chemical reactions in the brain).	A deep affection; contentment, confidence. Partners communicate and negotiate appropriate expectations.
Result:	Emptiness, consequences of choices made while under the influence of mind numbing temporary lust.	Security, peace, a solid partnership which can provide the ideal atmosphere to raise confident secure children.
Effect:	Being controlled by brain chemistry, not the heart, loss of ability to make rational evaluations of what is true, valuable and worthy.	Contentment, stability
Interdependency:	Cannot be sustained without some portion of love and physical attraction, always desire to be close to that person at any cost.	Partnership. Can lead to codependency if not tempered with self-awareness and self-guidedness.
Time Period:	Takes off fast and furious like a spark in dry grass burns out quickly and can leave feelings of emptiness.	It will deepen with the passage of time.
Commitment:	This is temporary in life and goes off after some period.	This is permanent commitment and stays throughout the life.
Bottom Line:	Infatuation is delusional.	Love is unconditional.

https://timeoutwithoke.wordpress.com/2013/07/15/
are-you-really-in-love-with-himher-or-is-it-infatuation/

Self-Reflections

The Love Chart

- Where do you fit in the love chart?

_____
_____
_____
_____
_____
_____
_____
_____
_____
_____
_____
_____
_____

Intimacy

Sex—the ties that bind.

Where are you in your life regarding sex and intimacy? We all are at various points regarding our sexuality. Do you believe that chemistry is something organic that two people naturally have or don't? Or is it the something that is developed in a relationship as you get to know someone and grow to love her?

The zing, the attraction you get when you look into her eyes, her smile, voice, the way she carries herself, the way she smells—all of these are personal preferences. Each relationship we have may bring new and interesting types of chemistry.

Your feelings regarding sex will be very different as an inexperienced young lesbian just coming out than as an adult woman with many dates and relationships in the past. My needs and views have changed regarding what I am looking for in a relationship. That's natural; as we mature, our communication, friendship, and intimacy also evolve.

Each of us comes with a variety of experiences. Was your first intimate relationship with a man or woman? Were you bi-sexual, transgender, married, unsure of your sexuality? Or did you always know you were a lesbian? We all have our stories. Our stories impact our perspectives and needs regarding sex and intimacy.

When you approach sex and intimacy during your dating experiences, each relationship and woman should be treated as an individual. We all have had past experiences and we all have preferences. Knowing this helps us to be open to a new journey. Together, you can explore what each of you likes and incorporate that into this new relationship. There will be various nuances to each new woman regarding intimacy and sex.

Another important aspect is "safe sex." In the heat of the moment or after a couple of drinks, your inhabitations might be lowered. These circumstances increase your risk of exposure to sexually transmitted diseases.

Has she had multiple partners? This information should be shared prior to being intimate so that you know whether you need to take precautions. Always keep in mind that there are two of you, and someone's personal health could be altered because of an impulsive act.

What Turns You on Sexually?

For each to know and both to explore ...

There are a variety of ways to express intimacy and sexuality in a relationship. Share and experience what turns you both on! What is your definition of kinky? We all have a little kinky in each of us. The question is, how do we bring this out?

Let's Discuss Toys

How do you bring up sex toys? If you enjoy them and you are not sure if she likes them, without getting too personal about her past relationships, ask if she has had any experiences with them. You can break the ice by telling a funny story, like the time when you were young and substituted a zucchini for a dildo because you were too inexperienced to know where to buy one. Would she be willing to explore this in your present relationship (not necessarily with a zucchini!)?

Another experience is being a lesbian for thirty years and never using toys ... then getting exposed later in life. This is a very different approach to lesbian sex. I used to think *toys, dildos ... why bother? It seems so straight, like being with a man.* I could never wrap my feelings around that perspective. Once I experienced toys with my lover's female energy, though, they became a part of us and our sexual intimacy. Some questions to explore follow.

- How do you feel about toys?
- What is your preference in using toys?
  - Do you like to strap it on, or do prefer to receive?
- Are you into bondage?
- Do whips and chains excite you?

Self-Reflections

Intimacy

- What attracts you to a woman?

  _____
  _____
  _____
  _____

- How do you feel about incorporating new experiences?

  _____
  _____
  _____
  _____

- What do you think about toys?

  _____
  _____
  _____
  _____

Living Together

How soon is too soon?

We all know when it feels right ... or do we? The question is whether we are thinking with our heads, hearts, or vaginas.

You may need to consider this when you're dating and the question of moving in becomes the topic of conversation.

If you choose to live together, handling and adjusting to living with another person is the next phase in a relationship.

When first living with someone, you become aware of your needs for personal space, privacy, friends, and visitors. How do you communicate your needs? When you are first dating and infatuated, this is not a concern. Once you make the decision to go from dating to an ongoing relationship with someone, you get to know her true colors. By transitioning to living together, you have to learn to handle and accept each other for who you are, including your shortcomings and quirks. Can you now accept her as she is unconditionally?

A relationship is a part of who you are, not how you define yourself. You don't want to lose yourself in a relationship and end up resentful of the other person. Combining your lives doesn't mean giving up your individuality.

Time with friends, family, hobbies, and personal interests, along with what gets shared and what stays separate are all aspects of your life together that need to be worked through. You do not want to become too enmeshed or co-dependent in your relationship. It is all about keeping it healthy. I refuse to force my partner to participate in an activity in which she has no interest, but I do expect her to sometimes do things which may not be her favorite. Be mindful of each other, and learn to grow together. Some discussion questions follow.

- How do you feel about me having separate vacations with my friends and family?
- How do you feel about friendships separate from you?
- How much alone time do you need?

Self-Reflections

Living Together

- When is the right time?

  _____

  _____

  _____

- How will you each maintain your personal space?

  _____

  _____

  _____

Household Expenses, Finances

Money is a delicate topic for most of us. Before you move in together, you should discuss finances and work out all the details. We have learned this lesson the hard way.

My ex-girlfriend moved in, and I said she could live with me free for a month, then I came up with a reasonable amount of money for her to contribute to the household, including rent and utilities. The total was less than her prior rent. Then it became an issue. My thought was that this amount, all inclusive, was less than her prior rent, so I was dumbfounded when she thought it was too much money. This can be avoided by discussing money and expectations prior to moving in together.

One of you may make more money than the other; she might be willing to contribute more in the financial area. Is this acceptable for you, or do you believe in a strict fifty-fifty breakdown?

For example, a friend said that when she was twenty-three, she had a partner twelve years older who was more financially stable. The younger woman made one-third of her partner's salary but was expected to pay half of the expenses. Was this fair?

One way to resolve a financial discrepancy is for each woman to contribute a percentage of the expenses or a percentage of her income. A solution like this would have left the younger woman with some money for her own personal use, rather than feeling broke and indebted. She found herself always in debt to her partner. Was this truly an equal relationship or was this financial control?

An additional consideration is that there are times you can't be fifty-fifty; this might be due to illness, job loss, or unequal salaries. Being a true partner, you may need to pick up the slack. Having a healthy relationship means you are able to communicate your financial needs and concerns to each other and create an amicable agreement that benefits both of you.

Who pays the bills? Do you do it as a couple or is this going to be one of your roles? Keep in mind that, even if you are not paying the bills, you should always know the finances in the event that anything happens to your partner or the relationship.

Do you have joint or separate bank accounts? Do you have prior debt that you are bringing into the relationship? If so, how will that debt be paid? How will this debt affect you being able to contribute to the household expenses?

Financial concerns can be very detrimental to a relationship. Disagreements regarding finances can cause arguments and even break-ups. Either way, the bills need to be paid!

Why are we bringing up the topic of shared finances? Since June 26, 2015, same-sex relationships are viewed the same, legally, as heterosexual relationships. Lesbian couples now must decide, as the relationship moves forward, if you will remain as a couple with individual finances or if you will marry and mingle your finances (with or without a prenuptial agreement).

Self-Reflections

Household Expenses, Finances

- What are your concerns about sharing expenses?

_____
_____
_____

Ending the Relationship with Respect and Dignity

To thine own self be true.

—Shakespeare

Most of us want to be successful in relationships, but sometimes things don't go the way we want. Just as it's important to begin a relationship with respect, it is also important to end it civilly. Feelings of hurt, rejection, betrayal, and lack of compatibility are emotions we all experience at one time or another during the dating process. To keep mutual respect for each other, end it the way it began. What you often love about someone is also what you come to dislike.

The perfect woman may not end up being the perfect woman after all for you. You want to end it with as little drama as possible. The alphabet magnets that used to spell out "I Love You!" on the fridge should not be used for hate notes at the end, spelling things like "Move Out."

Again, remember that the lesbian community is a small one. You want to be mindful that we are all looking for love. Some of us get it right the first time; others take several journeys.

A very important aspect of any relationship is self-love. Never lose yourself in the relationship; keep your friends, family, and your interests close. Always ask yourself whether it is good for you and whether you are being true to yourself.

Ask yourself what makes you happy so that you can truly love yourself and share that love with your partner. Self-love is the key to personal happiness. If you take anything from this book take this:

In time, if you are open to the journey, you will find great love—but it all starts with you.

JUST LOVE YOURSELF ...

Enjoy the Journey, keep an open heart, and have fun!

Andrea DiMattia, Co-Author

I have been called smart, adorable, fun-loving, funny, opinionated, direct, and even bossy at times. I am a person who thinks with my heart and my mind. I am very good at making connections with people. I feel that it is important to make someone smile every day, and it is important to give back in life.

I hold a bachelor's degree in nursing. Currently, I work as a visiting cardiac IV/hospice case manager. My job as a nurse has taught me to value both life and love.

I think William Blake says it best: "If a thing loves, it is infinite,"

I grew up in Rhode Island and currently reside there among family and close friends. My grandparents, with whom I had a close bond, were probably my biggest influence regarding love and relationships. They had a marriage that lasted for sixty-one years! Someday, I hope to find that great love, and dating is the beginning of the journey.

Dating is not an easy thing. I know this firsthand. I am still looking for Ms. Right and have come across a lot of Ms. Wrongs. Dating brings a plethora of emotions to the surface—like the excitement I feel when I meet a new individual and wonder *will she be the "One"?*

There is also the heartache that we all feel with rejection. We all go through these emotions.

I figured, why not give some advice on the things that I have encountered?

I hope that it makes you brave, because you have to keep trying. Never give up on seeking true love.

I hope my advice will cause you to self-reflect—and, hopefully, date smart.

Loretta Becker, Co-Author

Life has been good to me having opportunities to grow spiritually and enjoying life to the fullest. My personal philosophy is that Love conquers all! I treat others as I wish to be treated with kindness and Love.

I was raised in Rhode Island by a strong Portuguese single mother that taught us we could achieve anything we wanted in life. I received my bachelors in psychology and my masters in health education while working and caring for my son. For twenty five years I worked in social services, then in training, education, public speaking and presenting in the area of health and wellness. Presently I work in pharmaceuticals as a sales representative.

I am blessed with two children and three grandchildren. I have a partner that I met through on line dating and together we are creating a wonderful journey together.

I have been out for thirty five years and dating has changed considerably over the years. As a young woman you would go "out" and meet someone at the bar. Now there are so many wonderful venues and options in meeting women and on line dating being one of them; hence the book was created. I hope you enjoy it as much I enjoyed writing it and reflecting on my dating experiences.

Lovingly,

Loretta Becker

Toon Perkins, Cover Designer

I am a "multidisciplinary" artist: painter, photographer, sculptor, and graphic designer. Art has been a lifelong passion. With more than twenty years of experience, I have the skill to make projects come to life.

I was born in France, and I studied fine arts and graphics arts in Paris. I have lived in Newport, Rhode Island, since 2008.

I am also very passionate about nature and animals. My French bulldogs, Atticus and Gatsby, inspire me in my artwork. I enjoy painting original pet portraits. I use different media for my work, such as acrylic, oils, and watercolor. I also use different styles for my work.

My hope is to share with you the smile and joy my Frenchies bring into my life and to reflect that in my art.

As an award-winning artist and graphic designer, I was fortunate to team up with an amazing company to develop the prize-winning PC action adventure games Fahrenheit—Indigo Prophecy, for PS2, and Omicron's the Nomad Soul, featuring David Bowie.

Additionally, I have experience in web and print design and have led many successful political, advertising, and marketing campaigns.

References

Finkel, E. J., Eastwick, P. W., Karney, B. R., Reis, H. T., & Sprecher, S. (2012). Online dating; a critical analysis from perspective of psychological science. Retrieved from

Houran, J. (2006). Yes Virginia ... there Really is Online dating Retrieved from http://www.onlinedatingmagazine.com/columns/2006editorials/02-onlinedating.html

Printed in the United States
By Bookmasters